Word in Space
&
Duets with Erato

To Sonny Brewer
for all you do
to promote Southern Writers
in Fairhope!

Fred Marchman
Nov. 21, 2008

Word in Space
&
Duets with Erato

Frederick Marchman

To order additional copies of this book, contact:
Xlibris Corporation
1-888-795-4274
www.Xlibris.com
Orders@Xlibris.com
38860

Special thanks to

Jane O'Niell, PhD,

playwright of *The Silent Bells*
& poetry professor
for her help in preparing these manuscripts.

—Fred Marchman
October 10, 2007
Fairhope, Alabama

Introduction

Poetry, true poetry, begins in the heart, rides luminous shock waves into the dark, and brings light to our shaking continent. Fred Marchman—artist, seer, gardener of earthly paradise, rishi gone-beyond, maverick bronco buster riding bareback his Blakean colt—opens a shimmering path into the visionary cave of deep-speaking Angels, that most holy womb "accessible but unassessable," that "Garden where thee Spring gushes," that place which, ultimately, we have no name for but to which we arrive in moments of trance (thus, "entrance"), or while moving body and bones in prayer, or driving the road in carefree, spirited Kerouacian tomfoolery, or during moments of solitude, purifying the soul inside those "Golden Chords of Harmony" that heaven occasionally grants us.

Like a spelunker, Fred shines his light down through rough-walled fathoms to make brilliant the waiting welcome mat to the "Heavenly Inn," the source of the divine breeze, the "Beautiful Wind," the breath of Heaven that lights the wick of inspiration and brings *shakti*-divine female energy—to "Thee Cozmos." Through his inspired song, his unique sole serenade, his unstopping middle eye, his fast-hand calligraphy, his pastings and pinups, Marchman takes us through the jeweled dawn, the sunwashed portals, along the path of higher consciousness—to give us entry into the "Throne Room" of "Radiant loving Holiness & Heartfelt Happiness." As the book opens and the pages turn, we too open, turn, spin and join the esoteric dance of an American sufi, a Mobile-lite, an alchemic maestro from the American South—one knowledgeable in the esoteric ways of Blavatsky, the poetry of Dante, the etchings of Blake, the lectures of Watts, the revolt of Siddhartha, the architects of Angkor Wat, the *Duende* of Lorca, and, certainly, the Swamp-boogie queens, Sir Bourbons of Honk, and steel-guitar strummers of the sultry thicklands of imagination's Delta.—Yes!

John Brandi
Quandary, NM
Epiphany (January 7) 2001

Word in Space

Contents

Introduction 7

Title Poem: Word in Space 13

1. Callstar 15
2. Into this poem 19
3. Into this Poem and Why... 20
4. Word in Space—Experiment # 2 21
5. At the Speed of Words in Space 22
6. Never Alone 23
7. In a Sea of Cosmic Light (etching: "Soulscape") 24
8. Marching to the Millennium (line drawing: "Return to the Light") 26
9. Thee Road (woodcut illustration) 28
10. Road in Space (b/w illustration) 29
11. Motoring up to Heaven in our Cars 30
12. A Message 32
13. Angel Fires 33
14. Write to Truth 35
15. The Power of Peace 36
16. A Ball 37
17. Worlds in flight 38
18. The Spiritual Emotion 39
19. Mapping Hearthland.. 41
20. Like the Wind 43
21. Start 45
22. Faith (Earth goes Home b/w line drawing) 48
23. Blazing Trail 50
24. Outsider Poem.. 51
25. Twist.. 53
26. Pass/Fail 54
27. Wasted Melted Plastic.. 57
28. The Art Gods (Angel with Holy Spirit line drawing) 58
29. The Naked Soul (line drawing) 60
30. Treasures of Time (Solar Logos computer drawing) 62
31. Treasures from The Silence 64
32. Born into Infinity.. 65
33. Star Search 66
34. Trailing an Angel 68
35. Space Queen with fourth dimensional mirror 69

36. Beer puja 71
37. The Crow of Zen... 72
38. Falling into History... 73
39. Downsized 74
40. Stone Moon 75
41. World of One 77
42. Valentine Comets... 78
43. Tales of the Legendary Madmen 79
44. Flower World.. 80
45. To be a Poet 81

Word In Space

First there was Space.
There where The Word Worlds were.
The Word was and IS The Sound . . .

Sound in Space.
The Most Beautiful Sound in Space
IS Music.

Music was the first Sound in Space.
Harmony was The First Word in Space.

Without Music, there could be no Harmony
In Space. Without Space . . .
there would be no Place for words
To have homes.
How can Space be Home without Words?

Without homes there could be no humans
Who have ears to hear.
People would crash like trees in the forest . . .
Silent . . . silent . . . & . . . homeless.
How can a tree be homeless?
Crashed though it may be in its own forest?

Without books & stories told down the centuries
Where would words find homes?
Maybe carved on stones . . . silent, but still seen
As words in some sorta . . . Space.

Spaces in which stones exist with words on them.
Stones as spheres which we call planets.

The Music of the Spheres is the Sound of Vibration.
In fact, it is the very principle of Vibration itself
That is The Source of The World as well as the Word.

Words are creative because Vibration as principle creates.
Thee Great He & She Who created The All,
Did All This through Thee Power of Sound and Light.

Words in Space are also sound and light creations
And which, in turn, create in new combinations.

Callstar

+ Mind the Heart . . . feel the Mind + - Wa'Dood
* Whatever inspires you, that is, effectively, your religion*—Dioramanananda

The Call of a Star

The star of Hearts is calling.
You hear it near and far.
A molten song of the East
Flows down to people's feasts.

The Edges of Time notwithstanding
Blowout paths from waste.
Tastes of lasses enchanting
Remotest places of Space.
And lovers who love everlasting
Regardless of Time or Place.

Calls to the Stars, are they heeded?
By those big bold beauties divine
whose numbers more legion than Urthlings
wield waves and wonders amazing
with sustenance silently structuring
vibrations both coarse and fine.

Yet the Edges of Time softly folding
Hold many a well hidden ace.
Like the rays of an army of angels
Beaming souls thru Time and Space.
Placing their orders for Purpose
And pacing the racers who race.

On into cycles unending
The orbits of beings unseen
Passing the dwellings of mankind
And watching the swath of their dreams.

Subtler than streams from rainbows
The Starcalls shower and flow
From Minds and Hearts & from planets where
Legendary Legions All go.

Upset souls of the cities
Battered and beaten from birth
Writhe in karmic cauldrons
—their home made hells on *Urth.*

But sacred planets still are singing
Supernal songs from the spheres
And the human dreamers are dancing
On graves of mistakes and fears.

For Time as you know, keeps unfolding
As sure as these thoughts seek to speak
And the Hearts in this Mystery called Matter
Murmur a soft down-home blues . . .
Forgetting for a moment surroundings
Incumbent with hard heavy dues.

Dimensions forever unwinding
Realms released and free
Where the Stars who wound us are watching
While our flywheels spin from the sea.

Casting our ballots for Eternity
We vote for the God of All Seed
Whose stars are calling us Homeward
And whose hearts are for us to feed.

For the hunger of beings is endless.
As endless as endless can Be.
And as endless as all forms of need.
The sounding vibrations of callings
Resonate with feelings that bleed.

For the voices from Urth keep on calling
And the zenith echoes with cries
But the petty conflicts of humans
Seem sunk in disharmonies and lies.

That Perfection Thee People are seeking
Is in their calls to the Beloved's Heart.
The Callers & Hearers are constant
with the messages that they impart.

With beams and rays ever golden
And spectrums pulsing afar,
The Stars return channeled refreshing
As answers to questioning minds.

Findings of expert celestials
Align all painful callings diverse,
Then beam answers back to the senders
before crises can curse them much worse.

So here is the "world situation"
Everywhere people pour out
Their hearts and their souls
under symbols on poles
& pinch their potatoes and purse.

Door to door & long distance
Are the callings—couriers carry thoughts
To the Stars.
Feelings of Love's wisdom-power
Is their gift that they send from afar.

So victims of lo-con hype, unite!
In your homes, in your jobs, in your cars!

In your Hearts all along
Has been buried A Song
Only non-neural nerds could neglect . . .

If you listen down deep
To a voice in your sleep,
You're bound to hear it real clear!
Its melodious shape
Permits no mistake
& its Sound drowns all forms of fear.

Concentric & stout circles ripple on out
Both whimpers and shouts are held dear
To the All-Star receivers & senders of Love
In this infinite network so natural and so divine.

But we Urthlings below cannot help but show
How our hurts cut clear to our rinds.

For the Hearts to be clear
Many minds must come near
To The Light that The Stars shine with Life!

And the Voices who call
From hiway and hall
Must beam with a stream of In Sight!

Their faces are plain as they proclaim
The things they feel as they creek like a keel
From inside where we're on the same boat.

And I only can hope like the bottled up note
that we float and forever abide
till a Golden Dawn arrives
when we ride with the tide
and unrole our Message on
some Starbeach Land & melt in the Hand
of Superbeing Selves: God Woman and God Man!

Who'll never need hide That Message, That Word
Which is always heard
Tho' in tongues not always as speech!

Thee Moment is Here
For Thee Symphony Clear
To caress every ear and attune each soul to its reach!

Then Thee Stars of Urth will understand birth
& the Truth that the Callstars teach!

Into this poem

You take your chances
   entering this "poem".
      It may not be a poem at all.
        You may ask yourself WHY
          did I commit to this so-called "experience"?

An uncertain land of cosmic confederate
   cartoon characters combining, contriving, cloning,
      honing & homing in on ashes from a trash bin.
        But a bean sprouts from Stonewall Jackson's
          stand in somewhere swampwater quicksand.

A stalk that grows faster than tropic bamboo.
   The Confederate Cartoon Characters climb quickly up
      as tho "raptured" from Lost Carlota, saved
        from the misery of exile, defeat, disillusion, despair
          to the Land of Giants they repair where
            Angels of the Confederacy shall bless them there.

Into this poem & why

Jump in feet first.
Be sure poem not over your head.
Avoid deep water.

Swing out on knotty rope
from tall cypress tree
Way over the cool creek
and drop like a cannonball.
Into the poem.

Stand on platform and prepare
to dive into the poem
from a dizzying height.
Twisting & turning
as you fall towards its
wet surface.

Hang glide or parachute into it.
Into the poem.
From such a distance that the poem
is merely a glistening surface
—a mirage.

Thus you approach it. The Poem.
You are where you are.
That's where you're supposed to be.
. . . But where is the poem?

Reflecting you like a mirror
Here is the Poem
Swimming inside of you as you
Dive into yourself.
Still.
No ripples now.
Quiet waters.
Where is the poem?

Anywhere.
Any poem.

Word in Space Experiment #2

Worlds in Space, Words in Space
Which switch would we wish?

Without worlds in space would we be
With our words where we are as well?

Dip into a well of endless ink
A blackness in which words form from
Molded oldness.
A land of learning lost and ancient.
Where a world of words await.

In a steaming stew they simmer,
From old memories we half remember
Drifting into present dreams
They float in puffy patterns from lost realms.

Some simply are residues from undone deeds
Or form the present life's unmet needs.
Others still insisting to be cast
From moulds we built a long time past.

At the Speed of Words in Space

Into words
At the speed of Space.
Into Space at the speed of the word.

Out of your room & into Space.
Out of your house & into your car
& out again at the speed of space.
Into the speed of words in Space
And into the whorls of that race.

Into what worlds in Which Space?
Into the place of words.
Into the World of Word.
Speed of worlds that whirl
Paused and perched pirouetting
Topsters.

Where is the top of a rolling ball?
Balls that spin
In a world of worlds within.

Words that whirl
In a race thru Place.
Words unfurl like flags to taste
The wind of new beginnings.
Then, leaving endings in the Inn of Chase
Lingering behind a veil of lace.
Seductive worlds of girls
Who grace a wordy world
Like fabulous flowers from a flowing vase.

Blooming stars as eyes and face.
Wordless worlds of seasons spent
Loving across the firmament!

Never Alone

God & I
Driver & passenger
In this plastic world
motoring in man made motion
pictures dancing jitterbugs
in our matter dream-show.
Yet . . .

God & I . . . never alone.
Parents dead to this world.
Tho gone, they are not alone either.

Brothers, sisters, friends
unroleing their parts in this
stagey, spinning top of a planet.
They are not alone either.
Nobody's really alone. We're all a-love
in these sparkling dewdrop worlds
where life is seen as a poem
& the colors glow with inner life.

Dogwood buds still sleeping . . .
waiting till their time
to enlace another April.

A toroid becomes a sphere.
A sphere becomes a toroid.
New beginnings in the Endlessnesses.

Nothing is ever alone.

In a Sea of Cosmic Light

In a sea of Cosmic Light
We move to where & what feels right.

Octaves away from mundane woes
Where we may assume a better pose.
Dropping off our earthly clothes
As this last life comes to a close.

Opting out of the fear & flap
We rest our hearts in Thee Mother's lap.

She offers us her breasts of milk
Unveiled as though by space age silk.

From her lips, a smile and song
Beckons us back where we belong.
Recalling some long lost romance
And doing some other cosmic dance
Another lullaby and sleep so long
On a spiritual spiral higher,
In anthems of our lost desire,
We toss our pain into a pyre
And gladly make new starts again
Knowing that there is no end.

So, caught like incandescent fish are we
In The Net, in a Cosmic Sea
For all this Great Eternity
Born again to become and Be
Who we shall as souls so free!

"Soulscape"

Marching to the Millennium

Thru these triumphal hallowed portals
We pass one by one
still wandering
holy hermits & hemits hankering
longing for the life we imagine to exist in
The Future.

A future fearless yet awesome.
Singing an ecstatic hymn & hern
heard by the hapless yet happy
herd of humans harking.

Forgetting fantasies of food for a time
we flood the Portals of Thee Millennium
like legions of lost and lusting lemmings.

Standing at the Last Platform Planet
before The Ascension, thus,
We wonder who and how many
from This Humanity
will make That Grade
at The Cosmic Graduation!

Return to the Light

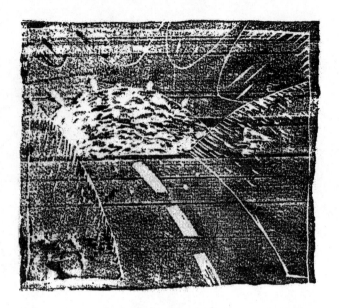

Thee Road

The ROAD, That IS
Thee Road that is
We Road, that is
Be Road beacons to us
like Thee come-hither
glances of gods & goddesses
gleaming with the promises
of Dawn, The glories of
This Golden Eternity!

What wonders & delights await
in splendid glories
of Mystic Nexus?

Pregnant & potent
are Thee Seeds for fabulous
& fantastic futures!

Road in Space

A Path too personal, perhaps
to properly perceive:
A Road in Space
uneroded, plunging
through those frontiers
beyond phrenology
to places we believe
from faces we must leave
from hearts who may grieve
sorted by that Mystic Sieve
that screens all sorts
of us, whether we stay or leave
. . . or return.
This sorting which in time & ways
shall place us
wiser in our wonder
& free from any sense of loss.
Then, even as now
when we shall pass
freely from place to place
free as Space Itself
Free as Truth can Be.

Motoring up to Heaven in our cars

We shall motor on up to Heaven
in our cars.
Passing thru brilliant suns,
galaxies & stars.
Surfing on our boards
arriving wave by wave
we shall strum Celestial Chords
& ford the Cosmic fiords
& feel the Universe
Has been well laid.

"The Duke of URL's New Used Car"

A Message

At the door . . . a knock . . .
At this sound . . . the shock
Tapping on my shoulder:
butterflies of thoughts.

The State of Confederate Amabala,
melted like Dali's surrealist watch.
Eyeball of some silent watcher
Atop what ethereal pyramid?

Watching the money-go-round
watch the billions of lifestreams
bumbling thru throes
of perfunctory Sun daze . . .
Whirr of weeks & seasons whiz
golden arches within wild windy wake
our Urthpath perceiving pursuit of presents
given so freely from where to what?

Our orbit folds behind us, asleep . . . now . . .
awake in the present,
we charge meandering
wildness as incumbent
jizzling cosmic waifs.

Angel Fires

Try to blow out the stars.
The angels will not let you.
Try to destroy reality.
Mind still remains.
The candles of Life burn on.
Quiet in intensity.
Atheists in what anguish-ignorance?
Thee Holy Fires Eternal burn on.
Blazing in all colors.
Burning without heat.
Blazing with the Power of Love.
Love of Thee Good gluing us together.
What fires are these immense beauties?
Hypnotic as mysterious birthday candles
They sway with a sexy yet holy love.
They beckon like the Sirens
only with their eyes & auras
you hear the sound of their music.
It is rhapsodizing . . .
Your heart lifts off like a cloud
& merges with That Thing
That's called Thee Soul.
You realize that Life itself is Holiness.
Lost no more, you find yourself in Wonder
as you feel yourself expand in Thee
Glorying.

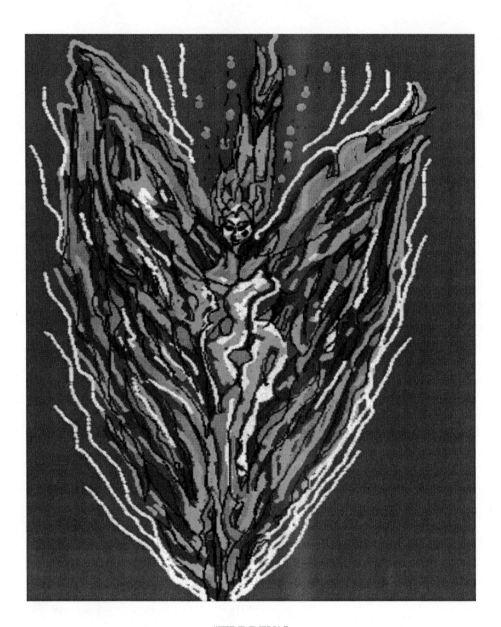

"FIRE DEVA"

Write to Truth

—A Rite to Truth re: our right to Truth

If I can write this poem
the way I wish, I hope
that It may reveal some truth.

Not necessarily All of Truth,
but at least some of it.
Some of Her—just a piece will do.
It will do.
It will do It.
Do It.

What is a poem but a search of Truth?
A search from self-as-Truth to more Truth.
What is The Quest but a path
blazed from where you've been and know
to Someplace Other you're led to go?

Mountain as objective.
Mountain as obstacle.
Goals are both.

The Power of Peace

"Heaven extends fully to the Earth plane"
—Babajii

Each Heart has a Sun
—a source for the Power of Peace.

Love is always Thee Winner.
Every Heart a divine gift.

Beyond all borders & waters
We are the world's One Club of Souls.

Our very own Universe unfolds before us.
All hearts flow & flower as our Home Eternity.

Greater than governments is Thee Grandest Plan.
One Whole Way freely given each of us.

We give back everything we got.
—no choice about it—God's got us.
We got God.
Who owns The Universe, after All?

Hands & feet & heads & hearts
All are channelling Eternal Energy Universal
without crisis, this is who we are
as you & you & you
& All that IS.

A Ball

—to Steven Crane

A ball rolls into a corner
of a room.
Nobody is there.
Where is God?
Is he in the corner with the ball?
Or is the ball
just all
by itself?
A lost ball.
Does God care?
Is God there
in the room
with the lost ball?

Worlds in flight

In a sea of cosmic flaming blueness
myriads of winging triads
round another curve in what cycle
as they soar in loose formations
individuals & families bonded
in the streamings of what driving
force flowing powers flowering
as they fly homeward bound
back into the courses choruses
caroling as they veer into what
vertical vortex visionary vulva
That Great Mystery Mother of All
in *alaya* who slumbers beyond *maya*
Recumbent, Thee Reclining Universe
to Whom or Which or What we give thanks
for this Glory & the tumbles thru Time
& Place.

The Spiritual Emotion

Choking up on the songs I love.
Choking up on unknown lyrics.
Choking up on the familiar
        POWER OF MUSIC
once so familiar, a family of
lost . . . then found . . . emotions
Now . . .
AH . . . Thee Beauty of It All.
How can I explain IT?
I can only feel it.

The Divine as comes
in Our Emotion: Thee One
in hourly oneness
Aloneness that is Won-ness!
We win in our seconds
We won in our one-nest!

One power is from that Winning
One Creator of Each & All.

This is, yes, another *bhakti* poem!
Spiritual Emotion from yet another
silent & radiating heart who wishes
Thee Great Cosmic Peace
to fly and free those that are bound, grounded.
They/We who are round, by nature, unbounded.
The Unlost, founded not floundered,
finding our selves where we are.
And being there . . . we are Here.

Everhere . . . Everthere . . . Everywhere . . .
We are as Thee Where that is
Everythere, Everywhere
Everwhen and Everythen
Timeless . . . Spaceless
Time more, space moor
we log our thoughts to Thee

bollards in sine-wave seas
Hour boats are Hopes
in this sea of endless One-Doors.

How many poems can carry The Spiritual
Emotion? More than all the possible stars.
For Thee All is ever-ongoing, giving us
these feelings we need & feeding us
such thoughts as we feel
can bring us into The Real.

Mapping Hearthland

In my cartoon reality
Are art hobos riding rails
hailing & hitchhiking roadrides
still playing out Kerouacian programs.
Shadows of nails. Surrealistic
Radioland imaginary dramas
Casting across emotio*nail* desserts
á la Thiebaud dumped into de Chirico.
. . . and here comes "Thietelbaum".

Golden rings of grasped success
still cycling just out of reach.
Societal carousel comically karmic
pumping strains glockenspiel
mechanical serenades to fallen trees
in unheard forests.
Anthems of Glory from golden machines
backed by paper trees
echo hollow audiostatic
in empty hermit crab shells.

Where does he go from here,
the barefoot poet?
One foot on an old steel skate
he steps into childhood's
red & black peachcrate soapbox
derby racecar motorless
with handbrake & rope-rigged steering wheel
He reeds his wet map, limp,
from Hurricane Danny damage it is
virtually illegible, useless, except
in the cartoon world.
& that cartoon world
once a riot of colors is now bleached back into black & white.

The pressure of time bytes
like a tick, its head
still embedded like Little Nemo
in the yellow world
of the cartoon reality.

Like the Wind

Thee True Life
is invisible.
It is Thee Force
Who moves The Forms:
We, wee forms
Beings with bodies.
Breaths from Thee
Creator of Allness.

Thee All is ever Alling
Welling up from IS
to That, to This
To Them & Those
& thus . . . as Us.

We are God's glory too!
This Cosmic Caravan
from Thee One to Thee Many,
Woman & Man hand & hand
Singing in Our Cosmic Band
from life to Life
from land to Land
thru deaths & births
We claim Our worth:
Thee Life victorious
over forms which die.
Our Eternal Source
is never harmed.
Truth is so much wider
than reasonings or lies.

O *Vac*! Eternal Principle:
Vibration—Great Vehicle!
Thee Creator of Our We!
Heartfelt hails to Thee
Wondrous Beauty
in All Thy various names & forms
& to Thee Life before & after
ever flowering into flows
of New Delights & ever renewing charms,
Hold Our Love within Your Arms!

Start

No matter how old,
No matter how young.
Every day you have
is a new start.

So start we shall!
Surprise yourself!
Startle yourself!
Start startling!
START! START! START!

Begin & begin again & again!
Time flies away into clockland.
Notice who you become without measurings.
For time is merely methods for measuring.

You become as you are: being, feeling,
existence, life as Knowing.
Life as being.
Life as bliss.

Where is a World for Our Souls?
Human World now failing as "paradise".

What happened to the Edenic Dream?
Open palms shrugging, struggling
thru throes of rowing centuries
Row upon row upon row.

Challenges of knowing
thru the incarnations.
With cars, without cars.
One nation, then another,
Here we appear, there we are . . . there.
Body building, Soul building solo
sole, con sol, soul building bodies
lifetime after lifetime.

No hope for lies.
No room for deceit
at the end of each lifetime
They present your receipt.
Debt & duty, booty and beauty,
balance, yet forward
balance still due.
Credit, like karma
ahead or behind
cryptic as action,
baffling as Mind.

Who needs me to pay the dues
for their blues?

All guilt is phony.
For all action is karma
that great Law contains all
retribution as well as your
contribution.

We are all welders & wielders
of Thee One Constitution.
Cosmic welfare is composite
contribution without warfare
confederate absolution shall free
both Southern & snowbird souls
from that albatross of phony guilt.

Permit The Process of psychologic Peace
to pervade & persuade our persistent
preoccupations to dissuade those
promissory notes we paid to our cellves.
That permitted us to "live" in hour
home-made hells where to hear the sounds
of Her Liberty Belles only drove us
further into Inn Security & phony onion fears.

A Chinese box with layers of oldness & newness
in the trunk of broken dreams.

Yet Hope like a single candle
lit in a window of opportunity
flickers like a yellowhammer
steady on altars of Our
Divine Devotion.

Faith

You carry it like a candle.
All the FAITH like ALL The Light.
Not extinguishable by darkness.

Eternal flames, Divine Sparks!
Those gifts of *saptaparna**!

Glorious still are The Quests!
Religious/spiritual artists, devoted lay preachers
For the muses.

Also glorious is The Remembrance.
The Love in a poem.
Warmth from a kind and kindling heart.
A well-stoked hearth in winter.
For autumn leaves must fall.
A candle hears The Call.

Thee Son shall take us Home.
Our Suns are on Thee In breath.
Thee One shall draw us in again.

*   *Saptaparna* [Sk.] (Theosophy) The cosmic pattern of man poetically described
     as the "seven leaved plant" indicating the seven principles of which we are
     constituted.

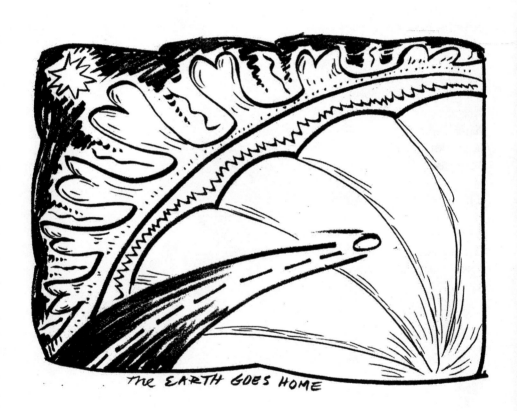

THE EARTH GOES HOME

Blazing Trail

Ever & evenly offering
blazing torches to twosomes
these guides & godlings
fill to flowing over
our cups of the hours
& there from their preordained
Destinies picture perfect
Perspective plowing preparing
Rich planets for holy futures
Tho they being beyond our ken
Are yet our most ancestral kin
Knowing that those roads are as reel
& golden as are those streaming interstate
Etheriums of our holy rolling motoring.

They gaze with infinite compassion
upon crushed & charred Trails of The Blazing
& glaze over ever so softly
the human pavement composed of shards
from charading hearts.

Outsider Poem

Obviously non-academically published
in corkscrew rainbows
where gorgeous goddesses greet him:
The bard from Backyard "Z" mows.

He hasn't paid the sin-tax.
In lieu of grammar he hires help
from Amor.
Armored with alliterative ammo: grams, grits,
bits, pits, he shovels silver syllables
with an old wooden "Ur Board".
He rolls the 3 tetrahedral dice thrice.
Esoteric to the bone . . .
He is the quintessential "outsider" poet.

Secret notebook of astral adventures
to de Nile.
Table fulla all kinda weird skribblings
in a pile.
Mystical symbols carved in stone.
Living in a Confederate jungle home.
Trysting with and kissing his desk model.

Royal, he riffs with the grey & white
mockingbirds. They are his friends,
or so he feels.
Converting
"reality" into fiction and reversing the process . . .
Ah! The alchemy of literature.
A vantage point Southern verandah view
complete with fantasy antebellum fixtures,
the outsider poet becomes Sur Bourbon
peering thru tangles of honeysuckle
squinting hazel eyes under the panama brim
gaze thru warping mirage
summery gardens mazes
amazed at intoxicating magnolias.
Lost Easter eggs in the monkey grass
memories of haunting hermocallis lilies.

When will he smile again?
When will he laugh? Where is his mistress?
The Blue Refrigerator
opening cool has no answers.

Twist

Twisty dream. Twist.
Twisting. Twisting the night away.
Twisted bed sheets.
Twisting up & down.
    Twisted d.n.a.
Twisted snoods
    twisting in the wind.

A flat horizon of surrealistic academies
    so many ambulatory professors
standing on twisted plaster pedestals
    under the bleak radiation
of a man-mad reality
    twisting in the winds of change
        hung out . . . hanging out . . . to dry.

Pass/Fail

Past lives. Passed lives
Passed birth
Passed childhood,
Passed gradeschool
Stopped @ Love.
Passed sex
Flunked love.
Passed college,
Flunked love,
Passed graduate school,
Flunked love.
Passed war with peace.
Flunked expatriate.
Passed marriage,
Flunked money,
Flunked career.
Flunked a dream
Passed fantasy.
Flunked love again.
Passed divorce.
Flunked sanity.
Flunked Life.
Flunked death. Flunked psychotherapy.
Passed psychotherapy.
Passed truth
Flunked reality.
Passed culture,
Flunked Home.
Flunked roots.
Flunked children,
Flunked spouse.
Had to repeat Home.
Repeat routes grade.

Passed alienation,
Flunked emotion,
Passed mind
Flunked love again
Flunked job.
Flunked job again.
Flunked job again.
(when will I learn?)
Passed career,
Flunked security.
Passed Hope.
Passed middle age,
Flunked middle age.
Flunked Hope II.
Passed Intro. To Happiness I
& Intro. to Sorrow I
Now I am suspended
between happiness & sorrow.
Passed analysis,
Flunked honesty.
Passed inferiority complex.
Flunked job security again.
Flunked self-confidence.
Flunked love for the umpteenth time.
(Dumped by the best!)
Flunked the financial test.
Passed blessed.
Had no rest.
Suspended nest.
Riding the crest.
Passed the mess
I have made of this enterprise.
The rise of highs
The trough of sighs
Entranced by swell of open waves
to avoid an expel to the caves
of the slaves.

Trusting Cosmic Principal
will not expel me as I exhale
& inhale & pass gas.
I passed gas!
Like I passed knowledge,
but I am only just doing o.k. in wisdom?
Or just getting by.
I hope I am passing understanding,
or at least passing the Peace that passes
Understanding, 'cause it hurts to flunk
Love so. Hurts to flunk Money too.
Where do we go when we graduate
from this World School?
Do we have to repeat courses
if we flunk love too often?
If we finally pass love
& ultimately escape schools,
then what?
Shall we say we have
passed Life?
Can we not fail to pass
to a higher grade?

Wasted Melted Plastic

A metaphor for our times.
A silent symbolic semaphore.
A simile smiling sub-sycamore.
Miles marched in others moccasins.
Good to be back in your own shoes.
Millennium mutating millions
as we wander inexorably into
The Photon Zone
bombarded by what varieties
of light from perhaps our very own
Original Homes?
On we go. Sure as Time . . .

A soulrise splendid & stupendous
that leaves us so astonished
that we fail to rescue
our android co-conceptors
who melt slowly before our
naked eyes like so much
wasted plastic melting
into what withered terrestrial,
tellurian torus.

The Art Gods

Will they come
& save our people?

There are those
who are starving
for those things we love.
we want to help them.

Who are those angels who
stumbled & fell
into earthly form
muddling in mundane forgetfulness
Lost on Earth? This Earth.
This Earth that is indeed in Outer Space.

We artists cheer when tyrants tumble . . .
We don't want to wait for Our Time
—for All The Time is Now.
. . . just as We are in & of This Time & Space.

Angel with Holy Spirit

The Naked Soul

Reclines in exhaustion
disrobed of lies
wishing only for that
Truth of Itself.

A pursuit follows.
. . . Arriving, it is a heart-shaped
ball of light
containing several wishes:
       Happiness . . .
        Balance . . .
         Security . . .
         Fulfillment . . .

—ALL tied up with Royal Purple Ribbon . . .
. . . now un-knot The Bow . . . and smile.

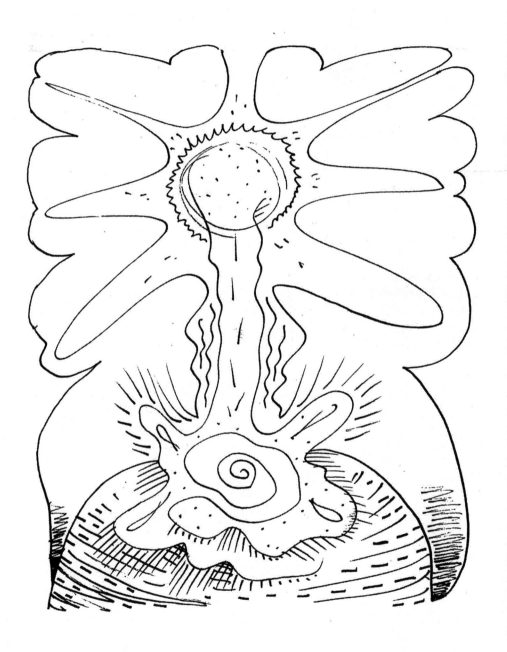

Treasures of Time

Illusory tho It is, Time is
merely a MEASURING . . .
cycles of circles & spirals
sunlight & shadows.
A time for this & a time for that.
In the meltdown of modern mind
what can we find left whole
bubblng in the froth
of hot or cold?

An interview with This Thing called
Self, poised between past & future
in that which we term
the holy moments of hour second berths
sleepwalking, sleepwaking, talking
in our wakes, creating such wonders
in slumbers we take a walk
on the tame side, the same side
following the wealth, That Treasure:
Awareness from moment to moment
ever moving yet still and seemingly awake.

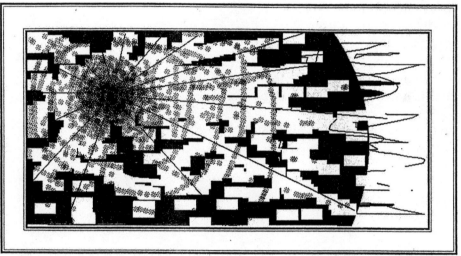

" SOLAR LOGOS II "　　　　　　　AV　　　　　　Fred Marchman 1984

Treasure from The Silence

Messages as tho brought on down
featherings—a treasure from
beyond the snows
from beyond What mountains?
The air of clear awareness
where thoughts travel untrammeled
thru the thinness rippling
thrilling our thought-worlds
where distance is in instants
as rivulets & inlets from
that Great Bay & Gulf & ocean
of our common planes
to which we label names & terms
and from these depths & heights alike
Move messages thru That Mic
depositing currencies daily
into our plowed & pulsing fields.

Born Into Infinity

THEE REALITY OF TRUE FACTS SLID INTO MULTIPLE PERSONALITIES OF THEE ETERNAIL INTERIOR. OUTSIDE ALL WAS STILL. STILL & WARM. WARM & ALMOST SILENT. THE CRICKETS. A CAR GOES BY. SEPTEMBER APPROACHES. HIGH SCHOOL BAND ALREADY WARMING UP FOOTBALL SEASON. SUMMER GRADUALLY GIVING IN TO SHORTENING DAYS. DAY BY DAY. A BIT FURTHER FROM THEE SUN. LONGER DAYS LEAVING. TIME & EARTH. TIME & LIFE. THE TIMES OF THIS LIFE. THE TIMING OF TEEMS OF LIFE.

LOVERS OF THE WORLD SURGE WILD & GONE & GOLDEN. "GROOVING SOLID" THRU TRIPLE TREASURES OF OUR MOST HOLY BEAUTIFUL UNIVERSAL ETERNITY OF SPACE & PLACE.

TIME IS GONE NOW. GONE . . . GONE . . . GONE!

NOW WE ARE THEE TOPS. GYROSCOPIC MIRACLES OF SPACE & PLACE DISPLACING TIME FOREVER BY OUR HOUR BY HOUR BEINGS MOVING BEYOND SPLIT SECOND BY SPLIT SECOND TOWARD THAT INEVITABLE CROSS WHICH/WHO LOCATES HEARTS & MINDS IN THAT SPECIAL DIMENSION APART YET WITHIN ALL LATITUDES AND LONGITUDES. EXACT LOCATIONS OF SPECIFIC SOULS AT CERTAIN PERSON-PLACES. THE SPACE OF THEIR PLACES. OUR PLACES. YOUR PLACES. THINK OF THE PATHS OF THESE PLACES! PLACES OUR SPACES LEFT BEHIND! TRULY TRANSFORMING OUR VERY UNIVERSE AS WE GO! AND AS WE GO, THE MIRACLE MOVEMENT OF MATTERS THAT MATTER. MATER MATTER MATTERING & MATTERING & MATTERING!

THERE WE GO! HERE WE ARE! TOP BY TOP!

EVER BEYOND YET EVER WITHIN THEE NAIL & HALO HOLINEST!

Star Search

Searching for our stars.
The stars that were our homes.
We gaze from zenith to horizon.
Searching for what fond radiance?
While that glow is all the while
right within the Searcher.

Qualities of ray-dance variety
like candles, like little lamps,
like laser beams, like lightening bugs,
Like black holes, like unseen suns,
like bug bulbs, like neon jazz,
simple or fancy.
Like smoky gods from the hollow earth.
All kinds of shines are we.
We are shoeshines, monkeyshines,
moneyshines, shining flashlites, miner
headlamps . . . a single match in the ink
of space.

All space around us
places in us our selves
where we glow to show
our locations, our places
in this universe of Wonder.

Grand galactic glories
soft pinpoints pyramids in paroxysms
before our rolling globes so blue
where we wheel in imperceptible dances
unkeen as we now are
to the motions of their musics.

We earthly stars have fallen, true,
for this is in Thee Plan,
Yet our glows are going somewhere, always,
only ever up,
Never truly "back"

Ascending into what new folds
of Mother Nature's Mystic veiling fan!

Trailing an Angel

My whole life
hungry in half-life
releasing radiation
active as a radio
famished, leering, lurching
for The Flower of That Angel's
face—thee one that got away . . .

Glimpsed in reality-clips
Longed for in broken dreams
Her petals float down spring streams
leaving the engine of my heart steaming
as muscles shrink & skin is withering
yet, feelings which will not weather nor wilt.

Still somewhere she sits or stands
or sails over long distance lands
Flitting here & perching spring
from fanning her flowers
magenta perfume my way
with wings of silver, gold & white.

She is that elusive goddess
or angel of Light.

Space Queen
with fourth dimensional mirror

Her longhand in her longhair
lost in a limbo of vanity
The Space Queen gazes
into her fourth-dimensional mirror
where she flashes into further future
unfolding moments of prolific flowerings
following what flow of feminine
principle progressions.

She emotes a note refined
as she enters the Space of Mind
and the clouds round her crown
can only glory as rays radiate Her Story
& Thee Message of Thee Trine & Thee Nine.

"Space Queen with fourth dimensional mirror"

Beer puja

Ablutions to Ceres, Goddess of grains and of The Harvest
All recalcitrant obfuscations not withstanding
Recondite implications rastacising
rasta, rasta, rastacising
rhythms of the dancing Shiva cosmic drum
musics from the dervish bums
the holy men & women bums . . .
For all who've lost their Hopes in life
for the divorced, the separated, the battered wife.
For all who've lost their self-esteem.
For we who've lost "The American Dream"
For we who pole or swim or steam
down These Rivers of Life's lost or Golden Dream
Let our hearts find Peace and rest
Let our care show us what's blessed and best.
Show us how to surf the crests
as we rise & fall through life's tests
Trough to trough from actions to rest.
When shall we take the time to fest?
Ablutions and adoration to you Ceres dear
Will You please wash away with your beer
Every tear and fear?

The Crow of Zen

Between my car and walk to work
   on a telephone wire overhead
      a crow calls under an overcast October morning.

Suddenly the thot: "zen poem".
   What do I know of "zen" thinks "I"?
      My books of zen are mostly gone . . .

With books of zen now mostly gone. given away
   Lost . . . unreturned . . . unpurchased too . . .
      too zen poor to buy all the zen books

I thot I needed . . . so . . . left instead with . . .
   the zen of everydayness . . . awareness itself . . .
      Being itself, in itself, My "self" in its "Self"

Yet what it is, the IS that IT IS that is, the Be
   in the thing Itself . . . and what IS "this Thing"?
      The questions have wings . . . O, life & thoughts . . .

Mountains are once again mountains . . .
   the "zen" preceding the scriptures of zen . . .
      scriptures torn up by nature herself.

Replaced as Always by Thee Holy Scripture of Mother
   Nature—She who gave us the paper, the ink,
      the pens, the pencils, the paints, the books.

Who has the "Answer"?
   I turn to the voice of the crow overhead.
      Why should a crow have any answers?

Who's saying he "should"?
   . . . All the Questions & All the Answers . . .
      rolled into One Ball—just like "zen".

Falling into History

One life after another
silent as pins
dropping in a vacuum
The Meaning of One Little Life
dropping into history
like a golden leaf
sailing thru autumn
settling and setting itself
among the rest
falling into rest with the rest
tired, tested, teary, trembling, tenuous
generic, geriatric
ubiquitous, anonymous
Life upon life
leaf upon leaf
turning what cosmic pages
in the Book of Life
somewhere, somehow recorded
in not only every fallen sparrow
but every hapless, hopeless, helpless human
who fell silently, ever so silently
into history.

Downsized

On the Day of the Pink Slip
The Disposable People will meet
in the Doom Room of the Inn Coherent
after wallowing in their has-bin
at the Common Euphemistic Congress of Incognitos.

Like so many "bic-pens" deigned as disposable
to rampant Moneyism, man & woman run
human manipulations & machinations &
miceavellian mash-a-nations.

"Living" in a puppet show
are the victims of most politicos.
Democracy it seems has truly fled.
Restlessly we try to sleep.
Broken families in empty beds
try to raise our sad heads.
Pinocchio nose. He knows
when his "would" shows.

Stone Moon

Cartoon reality crumbles
like twin towers.

Moon is white, not green.
people are blue—or turn blue.
& they are red & they are purple.
A lake is drying up.
Mountain stands still. Still sands.
How much longer on this planet?
Let us leave the laggards here
Since all they want
Is a stone moon.

Are you with me?
All the cartoon characters have crashed.
Only the ghosts of beige buffoons remain.
The rest are in Peace.
Resting in the peace of Cartoon Heaven.

A display of human dysfunction
Is impressed into the very atmosphere of Urth.

A key to the cartoon reality
Is clutched in one hand
By the astral shell of a so-called
"scientist", the cartoon character, Dr. Jo-Mo.

El Moderno, also in his astral shell
Talks to an echo in the bathroom mirror.
He reflects afresh upon the Deep Meaning
Of this Thing called Life.

The sun shines.
The breeze blows.
The Urth is beautiful.
He hears
September's Song.

Who shall share the Movie of His Soul?
When Love isn't working, the Whole Movie feels empty.
The soul feels lost.
When the soul feels lost, it yearns to sleep until the dawn
And New Rays roust it to arise
& once again begin to radiate.
Love that is Life.

True Love won't lie.
Likewise, how can Life lie?
Life is Truth.

World of One

—A one-world wonder

"When one person dies, it is not only he alone who goes, but worlds within him die too."

—Yevtushenko

The World of One is only one world.
Yet this is the paradox
For we are each many worlds.
Just as there is the one word for All,
All is not said in one word.
Nor, for that matter in one world.
The wonder is that one word
Leads to the next word & so on
To the next word-world
Where worlds of words unwind wider
& into wilder worlds until untold
Treasures fill the tills of the soul
And still the soul remains in wonder
At the infinite worlds which wait
In the Great Beyond within a world of one,
And one after one, words after words
come climbing to tell what's wrought
with world after world
within the worlds of One.

Valentine Comets

They crash to Earth
in clusters
slaking thirsts
of bleak deserts.
They feed the just
desserts.

They re-plant the plane
horizon with Hope
they burn, sizzling
thru Propland scenarios
singing anthems of
Thee Infinite.

Tales of the Legendary Madmen

—for Rhett Maddox, Frank Sears, Nick Lewis, John Brandi
& for all the "legendary madmen" known and unknown Everywhere.

From all over every Edge
    We come to Her Flower to dine.

She is always stoked with treasures
    yet always free. Free for the understanding.

Cross vast threads & grids of so-called
    "Time" & "Space": The Master Madmen march.

They rocket toward her face
    A beacon in a Universe of Place.

Sidetracked into sordid sideshows
    Some soaring sisters and brothers stop
      To scope the scene.

Or are they seen as simply seeming to stop?
    Machine Fate & Doctor God's Destiny Show goes on.

Back Home & out again to every known Edge there is
    They go!

Across . . . Beyond . . . & Gone!
    One hole cannot hold them nor whole them!

They are heroic they are legend!
    They go on & on forever—until they are gods!

Flower World

Imagine, as you gaze
    into the heart of a flower
        that you can experience the feeling
        that moves its very expression.

Lose yourself & find yourself.
    For a duration, you become flowerness.
      Crouched, couched in a twisted bud
        begin to expand in increments until . . .
      you become the blooming.

Bloom! Bloom! Bloom!
    flower explodes in expressing
      flowing forms of you flapping
        flipping, flopping forward backward
      sideways or shy.

Bold & glorious as mysterious ecstasies
    Of the joys of love as beauty can be.

To be a Poet

Means what to whom?
We are all in the Who
Are we not?
The Whole Who of It
At that!
Our entire Humanity
Humming of poetry
Our whole life long
Writing programs
& academic letters
after the names
do not necessarily
make one a poet.
It is to reflect deeply
Upon the beauty and brevity
Of the human condition
Within the play of Light Divine
That makes for poetry.
There is no "certified poetry".
A seal of gold embossed & a blue
Ribbon does not certify a poem
Or a poet either.
It is about one heart
Speaking to all hearts.
Calling from one epicenter to another
Like ripples from rain on a pond in the woods
Where trees may crash
While ears to hear them are sleeping
Sawing logs or soundlessly counting clichés
Of leaping sheep.

To be a poet is to attempt to understand
Or explain to others or to the self alone
The meaning and purpose of Life in The Universe
And in a more limited sense, this span of remembered
experience, temporal though it seems, in all the space-places
we presume to occupy or pass en route to all our wherevers.

Who can say you are a poet or you are not?
It goes with the job of The Soul.
The I goes for It.
The I being in itself already present as Deep Meaning
"goes for" yet even deeper Deep Meaning.

Finding Itself in a know, the perception of the Poet
drives a nail through the illusion
& pierces a veil that separates one dimension from another.
Seeking a communion with the First Formers
Who built this miracle myriad *mundo*.
So what is a poet if not a Who?
And where are the poets who are true?
Aren't all of us just posing poets?
Everyone poet-ing, even You—and Every Who!
You need no permission to be a poet.
Ya don't need no kinda badge ta call yaself a poet!

Duets with Erato

The Love poems

of

Valzdek Monetas

Contents

Frontispiece illustration: "Drive in Double Date"

Title Poem: A Hymn to Erato.. 89

1. Groovy Golden Goddess 90
2. The Last Rose of Summer 92
    Illus: Wanda Lust woodcut & poem
3. The Heartbreaker 94
4. Desire 95
5. Waiting for Co-Co... 96
6. Flying Life 97
7. Resting Hearts 98
8. Summer Candles 100
9. Essence of an Impression 102
10. Here Ring 103
11. Cosmic Belles.. 104
12. A Woman from the Future... 105
    [audio read by Mona Golabek on National Public Radio's
    "The Romantic Hour"]
13. The Church of Love.. 107
14. A Kiss... 108
15. Thee Heart We All Can Love... 109
16. The Fire 110
17. The Language of Love 111
18. Love Light.. 113
    Illus: "Dawn" Pastel
19. Flower World 114
20. As I Fell Into Your Poem 115
21. The Great Sex Race... 116
22. Goal Talk.. 119
23. Only our Hats 120
24. Second by Second 121
25. Not Dead Yet.. 122
26. Closer to Thee 123
27. Christmas past 124
28. The Poem in my Mind 125
29. Cartoon Life 126
30. Drinking Beer.. 127
31. Torch Song 128

32. Trying 129
33. Camellia Belles 130
34. Heartstarts 132
35. The Old Child 135
36. The Sad Guitar 136
37. The Smile 137
    Illus: "Hot Pie"
38. Where is Thee Love? 139
39. Pegasus' Hoop Dance 141
40. Lingering Libido 142
41. Hour Love 143
42. Lovelocked 144
43. Into the Moment 145
44. The Challenge of Our Time 146
45. Her Blossom 147
46. Her Face, Her Heart 148
    illus: "Vicki" (Blue Lady)
47. Spectacles of Absurdity 150
48. The Sleeping Flame 151
    illus. "Sleeping Beauty"

Acknowledgements 155
About the author 157
All illustrations are done by the author unless otherwise indicated.

A Hymn to Erato

Desires of the heart that keep on lingering.
Erato keeps on fingering the seven strings
Of her lyric lyre and all the lost lovers are asking Her:
Are there any sweethearts available
Who are not just for hire
Before the sexagenarian aerial ship
Stalls & falls into a funeral pyre?

Mortality, immortality, immorality.
No dues for the innocent. No dues for the descent.
Defer to the descendents. Desire in the desert. No dessert
For the deserving. Hermit cactus cocooned, isolated, daft,
Tossed on stones in surf. Surfeit of timeless truth notwithstanding.

Each dawdle or decision, a credit or a debt.
Default to desire. Feelings devouring.
Devices deflowering destiny.
The Songs of Erato go wan.
Venus with her vial of soma soothes the senses so subtly.
There are no filters for the philters of Erato
Whose lures of leading longings
Are like perfumed pistils propelling lurid lemmings of love & lust
From room to room or to dust & rust in an ocean of amor.

Season of the love bugs so suggestively stuck on each other.
The two appear as one—they are "an item" as they say.
Duets with Erato. Tarry black lovebugs splattered on the cargrill.
Of Erato's auto. Her charging headlites are instruments of seduction.
Her voice, her eyes, her siren songs that make us too an "item".
Endless are these duets with Erato.

Groovy Golden Goddess

Oscillating like a pendulum
Between reality & fiction
A virtually unknown cartoon scientist
Plays tiddledewinks with a shapeless shifting
Goddess in a miracle modern marimba band.

The tune is "Tico-tico"
And every cell dances as the golden goddess grooves
Over phantom pan tones
Which echo in a jungle of hardwoods.
She flings her Wagnarian haltertop
Into the tropic rains
& Dances naked on the bar
code of the Nude World Odor.
Her vast body of endless skin stretches across all natural borders.

In Peru, panderers & pilferers will try to tumble
Those tremendous ancient & silent stones that tell her story,
But only Mistresses of Music may turn
The Key to Her Mystery, meaning,
She can be heard but not seen, except, perhaps,
In the transport of some special dream.

Shall Truth from her temple be told?
Only as the rhythm of Love allows It to unfold.

In our dreams she shall feel us
Dancing until all exhausted
Have had their fill, & so,
Then, for the final thrill
We gaze in child's amaze
As she mounts her holy horse, Pegasus,
& thru the stars they go prancing in a blaze!

The Last Rose of Summer

—A paean* to Erato, muse of lyric and amorous poetry

The Last Rose of Summer turns brown, stays on its stem.
    A her waiting for a him, or a him who found no her to whom to present
    The Last Rose of Summer.
    The Last Rose of Summer has gone brown & unpicked, uncut, undelivered.
    Erato is waiting—yet who can predict the ways of a muse?
    Erato, muse of lyric and amatory poetry, unrole your scroll & reveal
    what blessings you may be bestowing upon the greying groupies of the
    Sgt. Pepper's Lonely Hearts Club Band.

There are yet more roses in the shrubbery
As long as Hope endures, as ever she does!
Love's dream may yet manifest, as surely even
As the fervid, torpid, torrid heat of August begins to relent
If only imperceptibly.

Rise Erato & show me the Next Rose, please!
Ah, those roses we remember to smell along life's way.
The time it takes is a pleasant diversion from the division of The World.
In an Eternity that lasts from second to second and moment to moments
Are preciousnesses. Precious memories. Precious realities. Precious life.
Lasting longer than the Last Rose of Summer.

---

[1]*   Paean= a song of joy, praise, triumph, or the like. Greek Antiquity—a hymn of
    praise, Joy or Triumph associated with the cult of Apollo & Artemis. Artemis
    (Greek Religion)= The virgin huntress. A goddess of wild nature who is
    associated with the moon, as her twin brother, Apollo is associated with the
    Sun. The Romans changed Artemis to Diana to suit their different culture.

WANDA
Lust

She's getting
older.
sunglasses
&
cigarettes
&
cigarette
holder.

She gropes
for a match,
she gropes
for a mate,

How much
longer
can she
wait?

The Heartbreaker

or

The Long Goodbye from Singing Flower

The perfume of her song
Engulfs the hearts
With deepest longing
Her colors mesmerize—magentas, fuschias,
Ivory and blanched rose.

The Singing Flower is not crying
As she pushes away another
Broken heart.

She so softly sings,
Sighing with each syllable
Surrounded in sound by a sad solo samba
South American, Brazilian guitar.

The pretty flower of her face.
Her hair, her head,
Nods in the humid draft
As she wastes another
Hapless suitor who would be
Her hero.

Crumpled in her tiny fist,
She dumps him, trashed like a wad of paper.

Desire

You want.
You want what?
You want what you don't have.

You have what?
You have lots of . . . what?
Lots of . . . Whatever.

You want more.
You want what you have already.
You want to keep what you've got.
You want more.
You want what They've got.

They want.
They want too.
They want what you've got.

You give what you have.
You sell what you have.
You sell what you want.

Thus, Desire becomes Service.

Waiting for Co-Co

A lonely toothbrush erect in a ceramic mug
Longs by the lavatory for her return.

A full pack of Marlboros on the white plastic table
On the treehouse deck lay waiting too for her lips.
And the little red cigarette lighter I bought her
That day I got her gas in the BP station.

The closeness that distance brings by means of the little things.
The distance between the closeness.

"I don't want people to think of us as a couple" she says.
Words like these can feel like nails.
The heart drops a note, an octave. The "nails" of love.

Endless longing, endless hope
Like a cartoon turtle, senior City Zen still hopes
That somehow, somewhen, that love can still come true.

She drops the touch, the kissing, the feeling, the make-up.
He drops the dollars, the flowers, the need for sex from her.
Delete desire from the relationship.

The phone lies quiet and naked.
Spiraling into a dual tailspin
Another affair crashes and burns
Hearts plunging back down to earth.

Flying Life

She flies into your Life
    like a songbird.

She perches, looks this way
    and that

She cocks her head
    & gives you a glance

You give her a deep & loving
    glance

She flies away in a start

Too soon she's a speck
    in the sky.

Away from your perch
    you are The One Winging.

You see Her again & again.
    She is also on the wing.

But when you pass each other
    there is no recircling.

Migrating from nest to nest
    seasons pile up like golden leaves.

October breeze scatters The Pile.
    Bursting forth in golds & browns like quail.

Flies the heart of a bird.
    Think of its feeling.

The hearts of The Lovers
    Their Minds in their Hearts.

Resting Hearts

When the Crazy Hearts
    have headed North
        for the winter

The Resting Hearts will fly
    from tedious brainland perches.

They will kool their wings
    in mello hammocks
        feeling The Flow

As Life Itself breathes thru
    networks of sense sings.

Each pore inhaling & exhaling
    that Electric prana current.

The Resting Hearts relax
    & observe calmly from a distance

The bizarre fireworks
    of blown bioelectric circuits.

The Wild Hearts blaze red & orange
    like comets plunging into black
        holes of burnt out stars.

Heated hearts try hard to fan fun flames
    to crackling incandescence.

So intensely They Blaze that some become
    progressively toasted, cooked, melted,
        burned & finally . . .

Ashed & blown to Whatever wild or errant
    wind or breeze may move their molecules
        remaining back to a pre-atomic

Simplicity.

"Crazy Hearts"

Summer Candles

—to Elizabeth

Roaming Roman candles
twisting like two vinehearts
soaring to such splendid heights
singing dewettes about the roses

sparking in the t-zones
talking on the telephones
going on The Knowingness
of what to say & how to dress
& address the Letters to God
& readdress psyche & Spirit
& undress down to the hungry skin
& start & stop & start again
& just end up as souls & friends
fumbling for some explanation
that can replace the lost sensation
of a romance blown apart with a sigh
as our rockets roared on high
& a "death", a goodbye, in my backyard
hoisted by our own petard

Sparks still fall and cinders charred
spiraling into what waiting fate?
Ardent Star-beings at The Gate.
Ancient highways crooked and straight
return us thru this mundane maze
until we find thru unveiled gaze
That One Who makes Amazingness
A Cross of rest of chest and breast
in this endless Search and Quest
for that Right Mate who suits us best.

Fire which flared in sky display
for all the world to see and say
OOOHs & AHHHHs is yet still one
& still o.k.—the candles burn
from night to day.
Yet there is always another day
& some new flame to light the way.
Cloistered candles in quiet holes
Pull like magnets to new poles
Someday to find those Other Wholes.

Essence of an Impression

Captured in a tally of moments . . .
The sum of her beauty.

Bottom line: love at first sight.

Love reclining nude
upon a violet sofa
nurturing Truth
in the form of a flame.

Truth as Love is Beauty.
Keats was write.

Here Ring

Hearing your heart
you let that resonance depart . . .

All the emotion it takes
to make an opera star,
is all it takes to make a moment
move in two thee
Heart of a star.

Cosmic Belles

Not to believe in them
amounts to anathema.

Miracles in form and name
include thee fabulous female forest of frames,
yet, whether in them or beyond them
lay starry lady legends in fame.

A Woman from the Future

At the edge of my bruised, gray heart
a new sun peaks forth
beaming what subtle radiance!

The image of her face
is not clear as yet
but I know she is smiling from afar
and gazing deeply into my eyes.
Now I feel that poetry is not dead!

On the dark & sad side of this heart
a soft moon appears
as a spreading crescent
as the crescendo of a smile.

She wants to be with me, I feel,
just as I want to be with her,
night and day as the spheres roll.

Next I shall hear her breath
on my face and her whispering
in my ear tender words of affection.
Now . . . I am her poem, at last,
just as she is mine.

She breathes me in like a moonbeam
as I exhale in the brisk night air
cool below the smiling moon,
my breath forms heart-shaped fog-rings.
These too she feels are my lover poems to her,
and so they are.

Her lips form a kiss to each billowing ring.
At this, my heart expands and thrills
in millions of tiny goosebumps
until I meet her face, where it melts and flows
into an ebullient fountain where
we both swim, spinning softly
around each other in full orgasmic ecstacy!

The night is made for love
and both our cups are full!
We fairly froth and flushed we flow fully
over one another like some sort of perfumed suds
and into our dual crystalline receptacles
toasting, tasting and thrilling.

This lasts all night long.
When dawn comes, we come with it
and feel the warmth of total newness.

We feel we know our future love-dream now
and that this is our shared and possible miracle.

At last we are able to live the divine duet
as our own true love-song!

The Church of Love

For the poet
The search for Love
& the search for Truth
are the same quest.

Roads of Experience
up & down hills & valleys
thru forests of confusion
& into a glen
open then to find Thee
Friend

Who helps the heart
& mind to mend
in the open air
where the Church of Love
& Truth can blend.

Down the river
around the bend
alleluia choruses
& echoing amens
a soulland of love
with endless begins
and beginningless endlessnesses.
. . . & a Then & then again
we find Thee
Friends.

A Kiss

God is watching
as our lips meet.

Hers on His, gods/goddesses.
Pre-sex, Post-sex.
The Eternal Thing still.
Still Here, Still There
Right where we left It.

Like some beloved lost object.
Lost and then found once again.
Thee only speech a deep sigh
as hearts meld in fixed gaze
nights and days flip like calendar pages
in old black & white movies.

Is love coming true?

Thee Heart We All Can Love

It's The Heart with the ears.
It's The Heart that listens.
The Men's Hearts and The Women's Hearts.
You listen to their story.
You tell your own.
You are alone with Them
. . . and their Hearts.
On a porch of a May evening, late.
with fan slowly turning to fan the bugs
away from you & your wineglass.
and the lasses and the laddies
speak of goodies and buddies & of
The Common Heart we all can love
that listens like a cartoon dove
who harks to every feeling
that drops like Groucho's duck
from the ceiling right down thru All
The Wheeling Circles of Our Love
Heritage of Our Monads
Comrades of the Duads
Trysters of the Triads
Quarrelling questers of The Fore Quarters
divining & dining in our mines
where we probe with pineal headlamps
and poke with forking rods
The Mystery of Knowing.

The Fire

A poet re-awakens
after a set of cycles
of What unknown duration.

His mind is sopping wet.
His heart is all dried out.
He gropes the nightstand
for his bifocals
& lapses back into The Infinite.

"The Fire" he muses . . .
. . . "whatever happened to The Fire?"

The Language of Love

Listening for that unmistakable feeling.
Groping for a vision
of her divine & graceful form.
Her voice . . . Her touch . . . Her glance . . .
The looks that tell all
(or just enough) to veil
Thee Mystery of Beauty
which hovers like fluttering peace-doves
above a pool of sacred neo-classic waters,
Thee Holy of Holies, continually pumping
iridescent photo-glories
where the well-whelmed heart
throbs nervously speechless & shy before . . .
before Thee Object of Its Desire.

"Dawn" Pastel

Love Light

Luckless @ Love?
Lacklustre Light?

Like Light
Love lights!

Like love
Light Love!

Lightly light Love
Lite, liter, litest!

Love like Light!
Light likes Love!

Flower World

Imagine, as you gaze
  into the heart of a flower
    that you can experience the feeling
      that moves its very expression.

Lose yourself & find yourself.
  For a duration, you become flowerness.
    Crouched, couched in a twisted bud
      begin to expand in increments until . . .
        you become the blooming.

Bloom! Bloom! Bloom!
  The flower explodes in expressing
    flowing forms of you flapping
      flipping, flopping forward backward
        sideways or shy.

Bold & glorious as mysterious ecstasies
  of the joys of love as beauty can be.

As I Fell into Your Poem

I fell into myself. Living in suspended disbelief . . .
Projection of an android voyeur . . . in It but not of It . . .
Free fall in the Land of Unknown Aesthetics.
Discovery of lost planets within landscapes of the self.
Expelled and expunged from three dimensional pelf.
In the space where there is no money . . . nor the worship of
Money. Pelf the Imposter. Posterboys & postergirls for
Bankscams.
In your poem I saw myself Someplace . . . in the glimpse of
An image via wordprint.
From a state with plenty of gravity . . . into what New Realm
Of The Dream Creators?
In your poem I forgot myself for some moments
Lofting clear and cloudless to a light on another plane.
Nuances . . . torqued emotions spiral like dust devils
Below this new vantage point.
Looking back and down with what divine nostalgia
I view the sculpture of my alabaster goddess . . .
She is opalescent, translucent . . . yet somehow solid
Illusion of material mass . . . all of which is irrelevant as to
Her intrinsic value. My worship is more like devotion.
Devotion and adoration as forms of Love. My love is
Veneration to Her for holding onto and embodying That Ideal
For Us All.
I fell into The Goddess' poem. The poem of Her Divine Form
Like an etheric sculpture . . . a spangling starry lightshow
With celestial musicians fielding prayers like tennis balls
And returning them to The Goddess for transmutation or fulfillment.
Who can follow Her from this loam? We all want to visit Her
Etheric Home. If we just keep slipping . . . into poem after poem
Will we ever arrive at Her Holy Dome?

The Great Sex Race

At the start of a *manvantara*[1],
The Great Race begins.
It's really the Race of Beings,
but it's also the Race of Sex,
for it is the polarity of the sex-principle
that is the mechanism for The Race.

Poised at their marks,
the primordial male & female sparks
get set to start, and . . . BAM!
A blast of "big bang" jets them out like darts,
Spiraling *fohats*[2] to distant parts
on this and that globe we are poured and ignite
as life-forms, as love-things, as color and light.
as atoms & ethers and minerals too,
Conjubing & jelling from the sex-thing we do.
From the water, the air, & earth & fire,
the sex-thing of the God-Plan continues on higher,
as stones, as plants, as things in the sea,
as sponges, and corals and fishes so free,
as dolphins & poiposes leaping with glee,
as whales, as sharks in the deep dark sea,
then later as bipeds & birds
as horses in herds. As bison & elephants
move over the land, as bigfoots, as pygmies,
as Kennniwick Man, as Aryan, Atlanteans,
Lemurians in Mu, as visitors from Venus
and the Pleiades too!
And not to forget, we're in The Race too!

---

[1]   manvantara (Sk): Roughly interpreted as the Great Cycle of time, Creation from the manifestation of the visible worlds to the dissolution of them, poetically expressed as the outbreath of God and the inbreath of God.

[2]   fohat (Sk.) a theosophical term having to do with the manifestation of life as vibration, energy, "light". Symbolized in theosophical literature by the flofot or swastika.

This Great Race that for so long has been run,
it seems we've forgotten the One with The Gun
who fired the First Bang that started our gang
on the sex race thing when it was first begun.

It's a kundalini movie, the sex race thing,
you take off your clothes
and exchange the gold rings.
It happens in summer, in fall and in spring.

It happens while winter is freezing most things.
The sex race goes on from sundown till dawn.
It gallops in nightmares and dreams in the bliss,
It carries the lovers to the worlds of the kiss.
In coitus, their sounds going "squish" in the night,
and the hearts how they pound
when Love is in sight.

And the races are racing
in all colors and kinds,
In the white, the yellow, the brown
and the black. Maybe orange, maybe green, maybe blue
races too, maybe purples & polkadots and striped races screw?
They fantasize and lurk in the steaming sex stew
and ponder the point of the sex-race to-do.

Do they figger that the faster that they fuck, they might win
This stupefying sex-race that goes on till the end?
They're balling all morning or at noon and at night.
An Earthful of races a-racing this rite.
Rituals of love at the physical plane
—to hell with the bastards, the kids with no names.

The sex race is a race that no sex or race wins.
After crossing the finish line, it all starts again.
So, whether you're in the sex-race or whether you're out,
you're a winner or a loser, either one, no doubt.
Or you placed in the first few to cross the line,
or you're somewhere in the middle,
or at the end of your mind.

But run, well we must, for we have little choice,
the races keep racing, as racy they sex,
and the sexes keep sexing, in varying voice
the tales of our trials & triumphs in text
so the sexing and racing are going neck to neck.
We're racing and sexing like there's no future left,
like a herd of wild horses headed over a cliff
to a cleft.

We're racing all night red, yellow and white.
We're racing as blue, as brown and as black.
Are we racing to light or racing from lack?
In this race, competition may hold us all back,
for we're getting there, going there, it's a foregone fact,
however fuzzy, the map for our feet,
for the Maker who raised us must help us complete
this journey we've started on the cosmic streets.

Complete we are as complete we were,
when first the fire of creation occurred.
And as that outbreath that made mankind
shall surely breathe us back into GodMind.
and too shall She, great goddess find
Eternal Fertility to rekindle new kinds.

Goal Talk

A desire & a goal are similar.
We get to a goal thru desire.
We go to / thru goals with desire.
When we go with the Flow of the Desire
then the Desire & the Goal are as One Thing,
one process.
Divine Mind & my mind work together.
A girl or a guy gets up and says I've got a goal.
I've got to go to the bathroom.
We agree that she or he is in tune with The Flow,
for, when you've got to go, you've got to go.
You've got to let the flow go.
When your goal is to go
& you know you've go to go,
there is nothing to do but to let it go.
—and The Whole moves thru you
as Its goal to unfold thru your role
as a pole or a hole for Thee Flow.

Only our Hats

Black berets
   The artist's symbol.
      But what of "success"?

Second by Second

Second by second
    The Millennia approaches.
        Second by minute I live
           My one day at a time.

In time & out of time
    But not of time.
        Just floating in it.

Timing is everything
    They say. Really?
        Yet not All is Of Time.

Being is everything
    Consciousness is everything.
        "Love is all there is"*

Without love, consciousness
    May not have had
        The desire to sire
           Worlds of space.

"Axte Incal, Axtuce Mun"
    (To know god is to know
        All worlds whatsoever)**

---

*   The Beatles
**   *Dweller on Two Planets—Phylos*

Not Dead Yet

He sits upon his cloud-couch
    At Christmas. Listening . . .
        angels playing golden harps.

Not dead yet.
    It is The Festival of Angels.
I hear human singing
    Playing Christmas music
        On harps of gold.

Not dead yet.
    I hear angels playing
        Golden harps at Christmas.

Not dead yet
    I listen to human radio.
        Angels play
            Golden harps of Christmas.

A time for rejoicing, it's
    The annual Festival of Angels.

Closer to Thee

In front of the black and white
    TV. set in the bedroom.
        His painting of an ex-girlfriend.

This is as close
    As he thinks he can get
        to God for now.

Christmas past

Looking for that Christmas magic.
Looking back at blue life tragic.
Toys were treasures yesteryear.
Now they're only dusty objects
In the attic here.

The Poem in my Mind

Is stuck in Heartland
  Waiting for the breeze
    Of Erato's sweet lovebreath.

In my bedroom
  Asleep in front of the TV.
    Is the beautiful woman dreaming
      She is only an illusion in my painting.
The full moon enhances her beauty.
  Platinum blonde.
    She sleeps in my bedroom
      with me—an illusion in my painting.

That woman is gone
  I succeeded in possessing
    Only the painting.

Cartoon Life

Walking around in a comic strip.
   the naked personality
      in the primary colors
         of cartoon clothing.
            and who can tell the difference?

Zenly espouses the moon.
   They elope into tracklessness.
      A New Universe opens up to them
         . . . entirely unexpected.

No snow to cover their tracks.
   Yet who will follow them?
      As we all return to the Great Sun.

Adrift in alphabets & mindsets
   scholars swim to exhaustion.
      Which cosmic emotions
         can save them now?

Fort Mood. Mount to attack!
   Cannon, horses, soldiers!
      Storming the walls!
         only to discover emptiness.

Unoccupied. Deflation.
   No victory. No defeat.
      No war.

Drinking Beer

But can't get hi.
Missing her pretty face.
the bitch who broke my heart.

Had to take back my own power again.
instead of give it away
to one who didn't want it.

Here's my beef:
where's the zen in this?
And who learned what?

Knowing goes on & on.
Knowing is a process.
Knowing comes from learning.
Learning & insight.
Insight is seeing
with Heart.
Heart & mind work together
like an engine
like piston & cylinder
& fire!

Torch Song

When I can stop thinking of you?
   When can I have my heart back?
      It's still caught in the net of memory.

The torch that won't go out
   Still burns in this cold cave.
      Wondering why this flame
         won't finally fizzle out
            after all these months have passed.

Knowing that by now, no doubt
   you have attracted new moths
      to your flame, why then, does mine
         still flicker?

Still longing for your face
   that I failed to possess.

Trying

Trying to try is still trying.
To do is doing.
The trying is done.
All of a sudden you're doing.
It's too trying to try,
so just do—and be done with
the crying that comes
with trying to try.

Camellia Belles

Watching white blossoms
   below her deep green leaves
      a lovely camellia-belle
         does a strip-tease.

Revealing her bodice
   a torso so green
      falling camellia bells
         bury her feet.

Doing s strip-tease
   under the trees
      a camellia bush drops
         her pink chemise.

Pretty pink & white
   Blossom bells fall.
      Winter-green camellia bushes
         Now bare all.

Strip-teasing on lawns
   All over town
      Camellia bells drop
         & circle the ground.

Their modesty lost
   No longer coy
      Winter camellias
         Strip at spring's joy.

Camellia belle
   You're so risqué
      To drop your dress
         On Valentine's Day!

Camellia belle were you a woman
   Who once "fell"?
      Your pink & white slip
         Lingerie stripped,

Strewn in a circle
   On the grass 'neath your feet
      Looking so luscious & indiscreet.
         Passersby spy you from the street!

Your body bare is leafy green.
   Fallen petals on your roots
      Blushing pink & bridal white,
         Camellia belle you're such a sight!

Heartstarts

You see them in a hall.
you see them in the mall.
you see them on a wall.
you want to stop & ball
these heartbrake babes all.

They're coming in waves
they wax & they wane
& they melt you down again.

Heartstart dolls
like visions from your mind
who can you really find
in the world of roses & wine.
Like you, who are your kind
Like songs of ties that bind.
Bringing sight to those who're blind.
Their gentleness & grace
make you love your very own race
and they feel your sense of place
with fairskin face & lace
and they're so much to your taste
like some Venus from a vase
that you want to caress her waist
yet she seems so young and chaste.

That you know you shan't nor dast
as her fullness you now face
and with all her grace she glows
in her figure-clinging clothes
and musters like colored lights
and lustres, although you never
fondled her in her babyflesh so round
with her face so firm and sound
that your heart lifts off the ground
as you punch the jukebox sound
& your soul goes into lovelock
as you fall into nostalgiarama
right here in Alabama
and time-trip to some holy spot
like some reversed royal inkspot
cooking in her cockpot
a wild electric *shaktipat*.

The Old Child

Still playing with worn out toys.
The old boy pushes sixty.
Rather, he is pushing it away.

The toys still there
as images, as memories.

But they do not hold the same magic
as before.
Only the memory of the magic.

Now the old child searches for
That Lost Toy.

Call it love, romance, sex.
It eludes him repeatedly
like Alice's white rabbit.

A memory from early childhood emerges.
He's with his parents visiting a yankee couple
who are good family friends in Toulminville
in post WWII 1940's.

They had a big white rabbit.
He recalls pursuing it around
their large fenced backyard.

When finally he caught the white rabbit,
it emitted a yellow fluid on him.
This surprised him and he ran to his parents
crying that the rabbit had spit on him.

The adults all laughed but never told him
the truth, that the White Rabbit had shit on him.
They laughed, they never told him the truth.
Years later he figured it out.

The Sad Guitar

When my heart is sleeping,
so is my guitar.

When my ego is awake,
where is my soul?

The heart dreams.
It dreams it will awaken too
into the Dawn of Paradise.
The paradise where love comes true.

When my life goes sad
as it has for the last few years,
After my job died,
after my career crashed,
after my mother died,
after my girlfriend turned bitch,
after getting gypped, stolen from,
burglarized, ripped off
in countless other ways, ignored,
conned, swindled, manipulated,
economic-conned . . . what is there
to sing about?

When ever shall my sleeping guitar awaken?

"La Compañera" I call my guitar,
"My companion". She is sad.
She is sad therefore she sleeps.
She waits for my love to come true.
She's like Sleeping Beauty waiting.
Waiting for that magic kiss.

Waiting and sleeping and sad.
Wanting to awaken so she can sing
like a sunrise in the Panatal of Brazil
when all the birds salute the sun in song.

When things go good again,
"La Compañera" will awaken.

The Smile

She wears it like a jewel—it flashes
like a diamond.

It fairly glows
in the dark

like a phosphorescent chesire cat's . . .
yet, more subtle . . .

A waitress for the breakfasting buddhas.
She wears that smile
right into the lunches.

She beams it to me
yet, it is not necessarily personally for me.
For she smiles the Archaic Smile.
It is even arcane.
It is the Universal Smile.

It is the Smile from Outer Space.
The smile that traveled
like starlite
from a distant nebula
arriving and touching her
traveling through her to bless
a bevey of bluesy breakfasters.

Where is Thee Love?

What Is Thee Love?
Where IS IT?
Who has IT?
Where is my love?
Where is Our Love?
& What is Our Love?

Escaped into our auras
from the outside in & from the inside out
There, here where we do not see It
—only feel It.
We feel our love—That Love that supercedes
sex—sex which is merely division.
Orbits of an "orphan Humanity"
still cycling for the Whole Necessity.

Well beyond . . . wells dug well . . . so deep
into materialism that we broke her water.
. . . and found our father.

Ever as our lever, leavening us even
rising in the Wholeness
Wholeness as Holiness.
Songs of Wee Wanderers.
Tunes which tell our tall stories
Buildings of beings. Billions & billions.
A whole new universe of Us.
Going on & on.
Building & being.
Being & doing,
Doing & being thee doing-&-being-things,
& being This Doing that Does.
—It is The Mystery of Action.

Under my feet with shoes or barefoot,
This Planet which I for now, call Home.
Right under these feet this globe belongs
to What Whole System we hallow?

Beloved universe, This One we know of only in part.
A Universe in which we whos use
Thee Electricity of Love.
Thee Love that saves.
It saves because It gave.
It gave us Our Who
That is This that we are.
(Thank you fabulous *fohat*!)
So . . . where is Thee Love?
Here It Is . . . near . . .

It is here in The Where
Right where we are
And we are here in This Thing
as Our Ams.
And Our Love came first
from Truth.

Pegasus' Hoop Dance

Vaulting thru hopeful
Heartshaped hoops,
A persistent & passionate Pegasus
Strides ardently thru a rose
& violet shaped void full
of unbroken dreams,
he charges from one
rocky mesa-heart to the next
with legions of likewise leaping
hearts in flying formations
following flapping freely
on the beat of the Lovesong.

Lingering Libido

A blazing valentine
crashes like a comet
in a deserted desert
of cacti & parched sand.

The man inside
crawls out into the harsh
alien environment.

He erects a flag of Truth
& ejects an arrow of cupid's
in a great blind arc
into a cloudless sky.

Hour Love

A poem with your lovely, lively, face in it.
Centered in the middle.
Meshed with pixelated words, morphed,
a *tromp d'oeil.*
The Song of Your Life
emits from your glance.
The light of Love expands your aura.
Words in a poem unfold . . .
like time-lapse motion pictures
of glorious roses of all hues.
The times we are together in . . .
glimpses, glances, revealing
petals of perfumed truth.
Two butterflies chasing each other . . .
Perch . . . stop . . . breathe together . . .
Then . . . now . . . We/they gotta go . . . where?
Why? The mystery of movement . . .
Butterflies! Hey! Hang out a minute
on that rose!

Lovelocked

In your car
      your thoughts are of God.

At home your feelings go to Her
      The Goddess of your Dreams.

In The Garden, every flower
      is like a heart with a face.

Down Bienville St.
      liveoaks form a Tunnel of Love.

From the windows, leafy vistas of Peace.
      Mockingbirds trill with joyous thrills.

As seen from the mind
      the heart looks melted.

Into The Moment

This title for "Reality".
The "zen" of This Moment's Motion
and direction.
The notion of her face
as an open book
as I admire her look.
Her pages turning before me
like candlelight by a brook.
Her lips glisten.
Her hair glistens.
Her eyes glisten.
She listens
when The Pawn of Zen speaks.
The spokes of her wheel
turn faster.
They are "into The Moment"
In a Sea of Feelings
The Tide is out.
They ride somehow
The low and lovely lapping surf.

The Challenge of Our Time

Is to show that the Power of Love,
Unconditional Love,
Is *greater* than TEEVEE 'CULTURE'

And that the POWER OF LOVE
IS GREATER THAN MATERIALISM
& MONEYISM.

Her Blossom

Her blossom is everywhere.
Erato is blooming from her fragrant bosom
Her heaving cleavage leaving me
Breathless beneath black lace.
Her satin strokes erotic to the bone
At her curving waist & I am wasted
By those forms that make the shapes
and colors of her flower face.

Erotic in her presence, I am
Mute with an ecstasy intense,
melting in a lovelustre light-ray
sent from Her splendidly starring eyes.

Her Face, Her Heart

Her comic book heart
Expands in my face like a toy balloon.

Another "duet" with Erato.

I gasp as my own expanding
Is also breathless
As a child's balloon.

I'm singing with Erato.

Her face is like an exotic French dessert.
On which I dine in gourmet pleasure.
Then comes the moment of her smile
Which further blooms her beauty-treasure.

O, Erato, muse of amorous poetry!

I can laugh with joy
From the love in her eyes.

"BLUE LADY" I

Spectacles of Absurdity

Knights in white latex.
Victors wore vinyl
gilded with gel-tex.
Mediocre minions marched
in tune with jingling change
& the falling elastic "dolor".
Banknotes fluting neoclassical
columns of toy marbles off key.
Plook! Plook! Plooks! as childboys
lob them into closed circles of fantasy
ponds where they call "bombs!"
and "bombs no kill!" "Steelie!" one shouts
"Bohunk!" "Up-sies!" and . . .
who remembers the rules anymore
or when we lost our marbles?

As for the women, still girls in this scenario,
playing hopscotch.
They start at "Home"
& hop on one foot till they spread their legs
a few times en route to "Heaven".
Once in Heaven they return home the same way,
tossing rocks into squares, hopping here & there
spreading their legs a few more times on the way home
where they keep their rocks and jacks and balls
that they picked up or lost along the way.

As for the guys, they lost most of their marbles
trying to play the adult games in which their steelies,
bohunkers, cat-eyes and aggies were worthless against the
"Bonkers" and "Blue Meanies'" plots, the elastic bills & bogus bucks
intransigent vicissitudes . . .
a veritable vortex of eco-complexity
& unturned-off-key bank notes
sounding from the organs
of orgasmic organizations.

The Sleeping Flame

The long heartbreak continues.
Etching its disillusionment
Into enigmatic ventricles.
A chambered heart palpitating perfunctorily
—a pumping place among particles
Of Perfect Eternity
Permeating palisades of Pegasus' peerage of purpose.

How can the Masters of Zen
Amend this tutelage in turmoil
from a female Rip Van Winkle?

Like Erato, the lost Significant Other
drowses in her serene *svarupa*[*]
Full moon brightest in 100 years
Illuminating waves of her long white hair.
White as the death or sleep of our lost love.
Is it death or sleep where she dreams?
Only that heartbreak hammer that throbs
In her shell can tell.
Her eyes closed beneath winter stars.
She breathes shallowly the quiet air
Crossing her perfect teeth and lips
In a timeless cyclic rhythm.

---

[*]   svarupa (Sk.) means loosely: the cocoon-like swath that surrounds & protects
    the auric sheath.

The Broken Hearth observes all of this
As though by clairvoyance, and, although
He, Cupid's victim, is simply a spectacle of absurdity
He can leave no leaf nor tone untuned
As he re-reads some portions of his Book of Life,
A baffling unbound tome of trackless tonnage
Taking up trillions of units of Space.
Space he may no longer be able to rent, lease or buy.
He feels compelled to cry
Before the Altar of The Broken Heart.
"If you could not feel, you would not have a broken heart"
a wise one said to him.
Your Flame still flourishes
In threefold tiers, so let not her burning flame
Further singe your soul another bit!
Remove yourself from her heat and quit!
Go find another love-flame lit
That will not burn your heart
When you pass such tender love over it.

Sleeping Beauty, Acrylic on Canvas—Fred Marchman

Previous Publications
by Fred Marchman

"The Romantic Hour" National Public Radio (audio c-d) 1997

"Autumn Harvest" a collection of modern poetry, Quill Books, Bristol, In. 2001

"Anna Bleeker Eliza" anthology, Bristol Banner Books, Bristol, in. 1993

"Endless Sky" poetry anthology 1992, Washington, D. C.

"Sparks of Fire" William Blake in New Age, North Atlantic Books, 1982

"In the West of Ireland" "Tales of the Legendary Madmen" Enright House, Republic of Ireland 1992

"Beyond the Beat" Water Row Review

"Our World's Most Beloved Poems" "The Power of Peace"

"Stroker" NYC

"Premiere" Mobile, AL. 1962

"Beyond Baroque" magazine, Los Angeles, Ca. 1970

"Ecsay" University of South Alabama "The Death of Dagwood Bumstead" 1977.

"Comment" University of Alabama, Tuscaloosa, Al. 1962

"International Library of Poetry 2003 Poetry.com

"The Harbinger" cartoons of Dr. JoMo 1986-2000

Bus Station Blues—Alabama Photobooks 2008

Portals of Paradise 1st books publishing 2002

Ecuadernos—poems of Ecuador, (vols: I, II & III) Nail Press, San Francisco, Ca. 1969

The Four Mirrors Colonial Press, Northport, Al. 1963

Dr. Jo-Mo's Handy Holy Home Remedy Remedial Reader Nail Press, New Mexico, 1973

About The Author: Fred Marchman

Fred Marchman is a graduate of the University of Alabama (1963) where he took a BFA in painting, sculpture and printmaking, and of Tulane University MFA 1965 in sculpture and oriental art. In 1966 he went to Ecuador as a Peace Corps volunteer & worked with native crafts-people, taught sculpture at the Universidad Central School of fine arts in Quito. He wrote poetry & illustrated books, **Ecuadernos**—poems of Ecuador, did photography, painting, drawing & sculpture. He met John Brandi & Gioia Tama who were also artists & poets. In 1968, Marchman started the Nail Press in San Francisco, California, for the purpose of self-publishing in that venerable tradition of William Blake et. al. In 1973 the Nail Press was relocated to rural New Mexico where the Brandi's lived. Although it was only an antiquated (1903) mimeograph machine, numerous books of poetry were issued on it and new poets & writers were included under John Brandi's new auspices, it then became known as the Tooth of Time Press. In 1973, he published **Dr. Jo-Mo's Handy Holy Home Remedy Remedial Reader.**

Marchman, although largely a visual artist, (he has taught drawing and painting at Faulkner State College in Fairhope, Alabama since 2003) he has continued to publish poetry and some short fiction in various anthologies, has written art reviews and drawn cartoon strips (*Dr. Jo-Mo, Modern Plastic*) in the alternative newspaper, "*Harbinger*" (www.harbinger.com). He taught visual art and art history at the Alabama School of Math and Science from

1992-1995. He periodically reads poetry at the Carpe Diem coffeehouse in Mobile where he lived after returning to his hometown in 1979.

Presently, he is attempting to publish manuscripts from recent decades that have not yet seen print in book form, namely, *Dr. Jo-Mo's Nail Dictionary* (a lexicon of consciousness), *the Crazy Hotel* (fiction), **Word in Space and Duets with Erato** (poetry), and **Modern Plastic** (collected cartoons).